A Sense of Science

Exploring Forces

Claire Llewellyn

SEA-TO-SEA
Mankato Collingwood London

This edition first published in 2009 by
Sea-to-Sea Publications
Distributed by Black Rabbit Books
P.O. Box 3263
Mankato, Minnesota 56002

Printed in China

Library of Congress
Cataloging-in-Publication Data:

Llewellyn, Claire.
  Exploring forces / Claire Llewellyn.
    p. cm. -- (A sense of science)
  Summary: "A simple exploration of forces
that covers movement, pushes and pulls, and
natural forces like wind and water, encouraging
observation of the natural world. Includes
activities"--Provided by publisher.
  Includes index.
  ISBN 978-1-59771-128-9
  1. Force and energy--Juvenile literature.
2. Motion--Juvenile literature. I. Title.
  QC73.4.L46 2009
  531'.6--dc22
                              2008007328

9 8 7 6 5 4 3 2

Published by arrangement with the
Watts Publishing Group Ltd, London.

Editor: Jeremy Smith
Art Director: Jonathan Hair
Design: Matthew Lilly
Cover and design concept:
Jonathan Hair

Photograph credits:
Steve Shott except
Alamy: 9t, 11b,
18-19 all.
Corbis: 10b, 12b.
istockphoto: 8, 20, 21b,
24, 25t, 25b, 26-27 all.

Contents

On the move

Our body can move in many ways.

We can lift our legs up and down.

Our head nods
up and down.

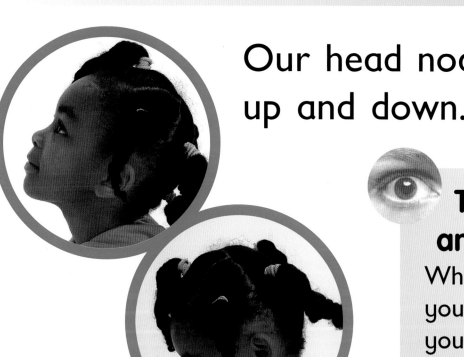

**Twist
and shake**
Which parts of
your body can
you twist, turn,
wiggle, bend, or
shake?

We can
make a
circle with
our arm.

How does it move?

Things around us can move, too.

A gate swings backward and forward.

Look and find

Look around your house. What moves up and down or around and around or backward and forward?

A wheel
turns around
and around.

A zipper
goes up and
down.

Push it!

Many things move when we give them a push.

Pan play

Hold two saucepan lids in your hands. What happens if you push them together?

A door opens with a push.

We push a
wheelbarrow.

We push
a swing.

Pull it!

Many things
move when we
give them a pull.

Glug, glug
Fill the bathroom
sink with some water.
What happens if you
pull the plug?

A drawer
opens with a pull.

We pull
an apple off
a tree.

This tractor is pulling machinery.

Getting started

Pushes and pulls are called forces.

Get moving

Can you find three things that need a pull to move, and three that need a push?

You need a force to get things moving.

Push! The truck is
moving now.

Pull!
Now the
puppet is
dancing!

Big or small

A force can be
big or small.

A small push
makes the ball
moves slowly.

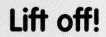

Lift off!
Find two bags. Fill one with cans of
food or potatoes. Which bag is easier to
lift? Which needs a bigger force?

A bigger push makes the ball move faster.

It moves farther too. Crash!

On the turn

You need a force to make things turn.

Pulling the wheel turns the toy car.

Pulling on the wheel steers the toy car around this corner.

Car play

Roll a toy car across the floor. Can you make it turn a corner? How?

AA 01

Slowing down

You need a force to slow things down.

Up, up, and away

How would you stop a balloon from floating away?

Pull!

The dog slows down if you pull on the leash.

A push with your foot stops the ball.

Push!

We should never try to stop heavy things. They can hurt us.

Be careful! Some things are just too heavy to stop!

Squash and stretch

A force
can make things
change shape.

Push!

If you sit on a beanbag,
you squash it.

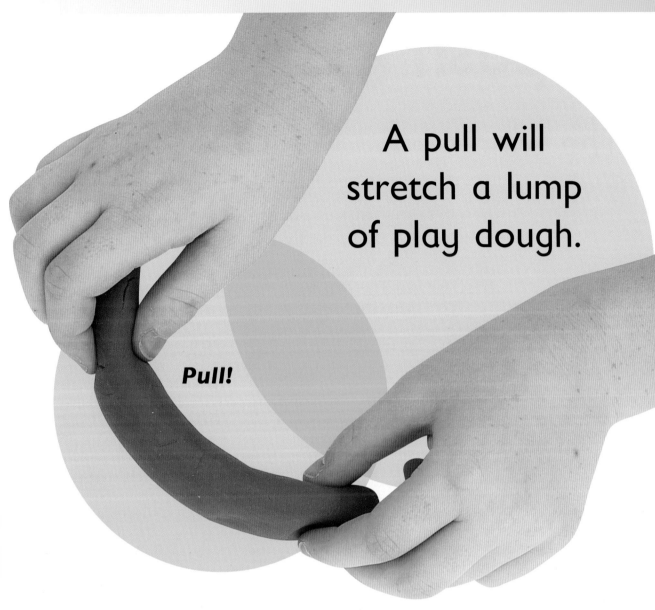

A pull will stretch a lump of play dough.

Pull!

Pulling and pushing make the play dough change shape.

What a squash!

What happens when you squash a bath sponge with your hand? What happens when you let it go?

The push of the wind

The wind
is a force.

Puff, puff
Blow on your
fingers. What
can you feel?
What can you
feel when you
stop blowing?

It can push a boat over the water.

It pushes the laundry on the line.

It can push a
windmill
around.

It lifts
a kite into
the air.

The force of water

Moving water
is a force.

It can push a
wheel around.

Water play

Turn on the faucet—first gently, then
quickly. What changes can you hear?
What changes can you see and feel?

The river pushes
the logs along.

The sea is pushing the sand castle down.

Glossary

Force
A push or a pull that makes something move, go faster, turn, change shape, slow down, or stop.

Machine
A man-made object that makes use of forces.

Machinery
Some kind of machine.

Pull
To tug something.

Push
To press something.

Squash
To make something flat by pushing on it.

Stretch
To make something long by pulling on it.

Windmill
A building or a toy with parts that turn in the wind.

Make a modeling clay snail

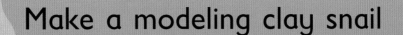

1. Pull off a bit of modeling clay. Roll it into a thin strip.

2. Curl the strip around to make a shell.

3. Pull off some more modeling clay and shape it to make the body and horns.

4. Push the shell onto the body.

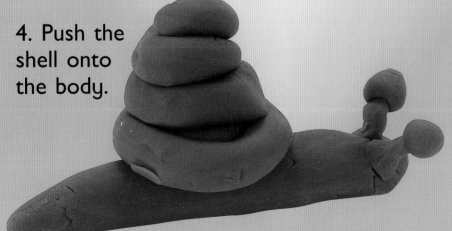

What forces did you use to make the snail?

Index